Basic]

MW00831792

Glenn Andrews

CONTENTS

Introduction

Bread's my greatest weakness. There are worse ones, I know, though most of them don't show up on your hips the way bread can.

There's something so elemental about a good bread. It's satisfying! It makes you feel well fed. And if it's a bread you've made yourself, you also feel a lovely sense of gratification. In addition, you can make breads you'll never find in any store or bakery — and, of course, you can brag to your friends.

Here you'll find basic breads — white, whole wheat, and so on — and also some variations and specialty breads. Almost all are made with yeast; most are basic breads of one sort or another. Two (Cinnamon Raisin Bread and Monkey Bread) would come under the heading of sweet breads.

For those who aren't fond of kneading, there are some "batter breads," yeast breads that do not require any muscle-building exercise. (Some cherish the kneading process as a way to get rid of anxieties or frustrations, or at the very least to build their biceps. Others — and these are the ones who buy breadmakers and food processors — are fond of any way of making things easier.) And finally, there's Kaleidoscope Bread, an amazing concoction that proves that not all great breads are leavened.

But first you'll find a description of the key ingredients used in breadmaking and a section on bread-making techniques.

At the very end, you'll find a few sources for grains, flours, mills, and all sort of other things that'll come in handy for the breadmaking cook.

Ingredients That Make the Difference

The ingredients you use can make the difference between spectacular breads and those that are just ho-hum. The secret to spectacular is the quality of the ingredients. For example, most people can taste the differences in flavor among fresh squeezed orange juice, orange juice in a carton, and orange juice from concentrate. For those who really like orange juice, the difference is huge. If you are taking the time and making the effort to make bread, begin with the best quality ingredients. And freshness, whether in yeast, spices, herbs, or even flour, does matter. The proof will be in the taste.

Flour. Ideally, you should get your whole-grain flours (including cornmeal) freshly milled. If you're lucky, you will have a local food co-op or health-food store that grinds flours in-store and keeps them refrigerated. Otherwise, buy the best quality you can find.

Not all white flours are created equal. Even among national brands, the amount of gluten and the quality of the flour vary. Try using bread flour for your baking. It is richer in gluten. (The package may say, "Bread flour for machines." Ignore this! You don't need a machine to use these flours.) Other than bread flour, by far the best to use is unbleached white, but measuring it is sometimes difficult. Start by using a little less than the recipe calls for, then keep adding until you get a perfect dough. (See Kneading on page 5 for a description of a perfect dough.) On page 32, you'll find sources for various flours (millet, rice, and more), whole grains, and mills for grinding them.

Yeast. Yeast is a tiny, one-celled living plant, an organism whose role in breadmaking is to feed on sugars and release carbon dioxide. This process causes your bread to rise. You don't even need sugar, as flour can provide all the food the yeast needs to work, but a bit of

Gluten

Gluten is a substance created when the protein in wheat flour is combined with a liquid. The amount of protein in the flour governs the amount of gluten. You can purchase boxes of wheat gluten to add to recipes — especially whole-grain recipes — to help them rise better. The way gluten works is that it forms an elastic network (think kitchen sponge here) that traps the carbon dioxide being released by the yeast. This is what makes your bread rise.

sugar mixed in the liquid in the proofing stage gives the yeast a fast start.

Long ago, the only yeast available was in cake form. Today, you'll find it in that form occasionally, but usually what you'll see is called active, dry yeast. You can buy it in packets or (at health-food stores and co-ops) in bulk. There's also "Rapid Rise" yeast, which seems very vigorous. (Ignore the package instructions and just use it as you would any other dry yeast.) One package of dry yeast contains about 2½ teaspoons.

You can also find little 4-ounce (115 g) jars of yeast in most supermarkets. These are labeled as being for use in bread machines, but can be used in any bread-making situation. Keep the little jar, and all other types of yeast, in your refrigerator.

Liquid. Use whatever the recipe calls for. Water is the liquid used in most breads, but be sure it's good-tasting water. If you have to buy bottled springwater to make your breads, it's worth it to avoid any off tastes. If you are feeling inventive, you can experiment with using different liquids. Try fruit juice in sweet breads, beer in herb breads, or substitute milk.

Almost more important than choosing what liquid you use is making sure the liquid is the correct temperature. Yeast works only at the proper temperature, and it's important that the liquid used in the proofing process be at the right temperature. Too cool, and the breadmaking will be slowed down; too hot, and the yeast will be killed! The temperature you want is between 95° and 110°F (35–43°C) — just a comfortable lukewarm.

Sweeteners. Yeast thrives on sugar, so most breads contain at least a little bit of it, usually added when the yeast is proofing. Honey can be substituted for up to a tablespoon of sugar, but *do not* use artificial sweeteners! When molasses is added, as in Anadama Batter Bread (page 27), it's primarily for its great, unique taste.

Fat. If butter is called for, use just that — butter. Margarine is not suitable for breadmaking (though I have heard that it's widely used in Denmark in their pastries). The only exception to this rule is Challah (pages 15–16).

If it's olive oil that's called for, use extra virgin, which is the purest and has the best taste. When you want to grease a pan, you can use any fat you like; if you prefer, you can also use a nonfat cooking spray (available in most grocery stores).

Eggs. Use size large. Using other sizes of egg can throw off the balance of many recipes.

Salt. Any salt will do, but sea salt is lovely. Don't skimp here. Under-salted bread will leave you feeling that something is missing from the taste, and the amount of salt in each slice of bread is actually quite small.

Basic Techniques of Breadmaking

The same techniques are used to make most yeast breads: proofing, combining the ingredients, kneading, rising, shaping, baking, and cooling.

Proofing has two functions — it gets the yeast off and running, and it's the best way to be sure that the yeast is still active. To proof, stir the yeast into lukewarm (95° to 110°F; 35°–43°C) water, usually along with a little sugar or other sweetener, and let it sit for 5 minutes, or until foamy. If you don't see any signs of life after 5 minutes, your yeast is dead. Toss it out and start over with a new supply.

Combining the ingredients is done differently for different breads; check each recipe. But if you're using a food processor to combine and knead, put all the dry ingredients into the bowl first and give them a buzz before adding and processing the other things.

Kneading finishes up the combining process and gives your bread texture. Many do this in a food processor, pulsing on and off until a nice dough is formed, then giving the dough a final turn or two on a floured board. If you have a heavy-duty mixer with a dough hook, you can knead using the mixer.

Traditional kneading is done on a floured board, with floured hands. Form the dough into a pancake shape. Using the heels of your hands, push the dough away from you. Then fold it over and rotate it a quarter turn. Keep doing this, adding more flour to the board and your hands as necessary, until the dough is elastic and has lost its stickiness. A "perfect" dough has been accurately described as feeling like a baby's bottom! Others have said that it feels like an earlobe. Doughs containing rye flours will always seem a little sticky, though.

You will see the phrase "a floured surface" in many of the recipes. Many of you will use a bread board. Others, a lucky few, will use a slab of polished marble. Still others will use a countertop. All of these surfaces work well. I'm happy to have a marble slab, which I leave out on a counter at all times, but I think it's mostly for aesthetics!

Rising. After the dough has been kneaded, place it in a greased bowl (but see below) and turn it around until it's greased on all sides. Cover. (Some will tell you to cover with a damp cloth, but I've found that any sort of cover works just fine — and in most cases is preferable to the damp cloth, because you don't always want to add any extra moisture. Plastic wrap or foil works well. I even cover bowls with dinner plates on occasion!) Let it sit in a warm place (ideally between 80° and 85°F; 27°–29°C) until doubled in size. This will usually take about an hour. A gas oven with a pilot light works well. In a cold electric oven, place a pan of boiling water on the bottom rack. See the specific recipe instructions for the number of rising times.

You will know that a dough has doubled in size when it doesn't bounce back, even a little, after you poke a hole in it with two fingers.

A further word about that "greased bowl" I mentioned above: This is an example of how dogma enters the world of baking. A greased bowl isn't really necessary, though almost everyone uses it. Some accomplished bakers, even professional ones of some renown, use a floured bowl instead. Others simply leave the dough on the floured surface where kneading has taken place and cover it with an upside-down bowl. I've done this myself, and found that it works just fine.

So although I'll be telling you to use a greased bowl, remember that it's not absolutely necessary. Still, it's a handy way to get your dough into a warm environment, which leaving it on a floured bread board or counter won't accomplish.

Dogma again will tell you that you must be sure not to let your dough encounter any wisp of wind or breeze. Nonsense! It simply isn't true.

Punching down. Just bang your fist into the center of the risen dough — this is fun! Turn the dough over and punch again, then fold it a bit; keep folding and punching until the dough is thoroughly deflated. (You can also turn out the dough onto a floured surface and knead just a little to accomplish this if you find it necessary.)

Shaping. Flatten the dough into a rectangle whose shorter end is the length of the bread you want or of the pan you're using. (Flattening it with a rolling pin is a good idea, because it will get rid of any air pockets in the dough.) Roll up the dough tightly from the short end, then pinch the ends and tuck them under. For a round loaf, flatten the dough into a square, then tuck the edges under.

Baking. Breads can just bake on baking tins or, if they're in pans, right on the oven's racks. But for breads that aren't baked in pans, it really is nice to use a baking stone, which approximates a professional baker's brick oven. These are rather expensive, though. So you might want to try an easy substitute: Go to a store that sells ceramic tiles and purchase some unglazed terra-cotta or quarry tiles. They're always inexpensive. They usually come in 6-inch (15 cm) squares, so if you buy nine of them, you'll have an area 18 inches by 18 inches (45 cm) at about one-sixth the price of a baking stone. Use these to line a regular oven rack.

Failing this, put your loaves on baking sheets that you've sprinkled with a little cornmeal.

Testing for doneness. The classic way to find out if a loaf has baked enough is to remove it from the pan and rap it with your knuckles. If the bread sounds hollow, it's done. If you don't hear a hollow sound when you rap on the loaf, put it back in the oven for a few minutes more. (You don't need to return it to its baking pan.)

Finishing the bread. Sometimes it's nice to rub the top of a baked, warm loaf with a little soft butter or some milk, since it will give the loaf an appealing shine. Another technique is to brush the top of an unbaked loaf with an egg wash consisting of an egg (or just the yolk) beaten with 2 tablespoons of water. With or without these touches, let the finished, baked loaf sit on a rack until it's

---

Making Rolls

Any of the basic white or whole-wheat doughs can be formed into rolls. If you haven't made rolls before, a good one to start with is the cloverleaf. Just make small balls of dough and stick three of them in each greased standard-size muffin tin hole. (Balls of dough the size of large marbles are what to aim for.) Cover loosely and allow to rise until double, then bake in a preheated 350°F (177°C) oven for about 20 minutes, or until light brown.

Don't try this with any of the batter bread doughs or with rye dough, which is usually too soft and sticky. However, those doughs, as well as all the basic ones, can be made into miniature loaves if you have the right little bread pans.

completely cool. (The late James Beard used to call cutting into an uncooled loaf of bread "infanticide"!) To avoid major problems removing the bread from the pan, first make sure to thoroughly grease the pan. If the bread then sticks after baking, let the pan sit first on one side for a few minutes, then on the other.

Keeping bread on hand. When the bread is thoroughly cool, put it into a bag and keep it at room temperature. Or freeze it. Bread can be frozen and thawed any number of times. But if you want the bread sliced, it's best to do this before you freeze it: Bread that has been frozen is difficult to slice.

Basic Bread Recipes

As you may have gathered by now, I feel that it's too bad that so many people are scared off by dogmatic rules about breadmaking. Bread is very forgiving. No matter what you do, the chances are very, very good that you will turn out a creditable loaf of bread. If you don't, it's not such a big deal. The ingredients you've used aren't expensive. Just toss out the loaf, if you must, and try again!

White Breads

Recently, white breads have fallen out of favor with the health-food crowd. But white flour, with its high gluten levels and forgiving nature, is a natural — and healthy — basis for beginning to bake bread.

BASIC WHITE BREAD

There are many recipes in the world for a good, basic, home-style white bread. I just happen to feel that this is the best. The recipe can be cut in half, but as long as you're going to go to this much trouble, it seems to me you might as well make two loaves!

2	cups (475 ml) milk
3	tablespoons butter, divided
2	tablespoons sugar (can be omitted or the amount cut down)
1	tablespoon salt
2	packages dry yeast
½	cup (120 ml) lukewarm (95° to 110°F; 35°–40°C) water

6–6¼ cups (1,650–1,720 ml) white flour

1. Heat the milk in a medium-size saucepan. Add 1 tablespoon of the butter plus the sugar and salt. Stir until dissolved.

2. Stir the yeast into the lukewarm water in a large bowl. Make sure it's dissolved, then set aside to proof for 5 minutes.

3. Add the cooled milk mixture to the proofed yeast. Beat in the flour, 1 cup (275 ml) at a time, then turn out the dough onto a floured surface and knead.

4. Place in a greased bowl and turn the ball of dough around so it's greased on all sides. Cover. Let rise in a warm place until doubled.

5. Punch down the dough, turn it out onto the floured surface again, and knead once more, briefly.

6. Shape the dough into two loaves. Place them in two well-greased, large (9-inch; 22.5 cm) loaf pans. Cover. Let rise once more.

7. Preheat your oven to 400°F (205°C).

8. When the loaves have doubled in size, slash their tops in two or three places. Melt the remaining butter and brush half of it onto the loaves.

9. Bake for 40 minutes, then brush the loaves with the remaining tablespoon of butter. Bake for 5 minutes more, then remove from the pans and allow to cool on a rack.

MAKES 2 LARGE LOAVES

CINNAMON RAISIN BREAD

When you've made the dough for Basic White Bread, you're well on the way to making Cinnamon Raisin Bread, which is a favorite with so many people.

1	recipe Basic White Bread dough
1½	cups (415 ml) raisins
½	cup (120 ml) warm water
1½	teaspoons cinnamon
3	tablespoons sugar
2	tablespoons white flour

1. While the white bread dough is rising, combine the raisins with the water in a small bowl and let sit, stirring from time to time.

2. When the dough has risen, punch it down and put it on a lightly floured surface. Divide into two sections. Roll each into a rectangle that's about ¾ inch (19 mm) thick.

3. Combine the cinnamon and sugar and sprinkle over the dough.

4. Drain the raisins and sprinkle them with the 2 tablespoons of flour. Toss well to combine, then spread them evenly over the two dough rectangles. Press the raisins in lightly.

5. Now roll the loaves one at a time. Starting at a short end of a rectangle, roll up the dough into a log, tucking in any raisins that escape. Roll tightly, but not so much so that the skin of the dough tears.

6. Seal the seam of the log by lightly pinching its edges together with your fingers. Place the loaf, seam-side down, in a greased 9-inch (22.5 cm) bread pan. Repeat with the other rectangle of dough.

7. Cover and allow to rise in a warm place until the dough has risen well above the edges of the pans. This may take close to 2 hours.

8. Preheat your oven to 400°F (205°C).

9. Bake for 45 minutes, checking often to make sure that the raisins on top of the loaves aren't burning. If they are, cover the tops of the loaves lightly with foil.

10. Remove from the pans and allow to cool very thoroughly on a rack before slicing.

MAKES 2 LOAVES

ENGLISH MUFFIN BREAD

If you're looking for a perfect bread to slice and toast for breakfast, this is it. I prefer this to commercial English muffins. (And it's just loaded with nooks and crannies!) English Muffin Bread is one example of batter bread, which requires no kneading.

2	**cups (475 ml) milk**
½	**cup (120 ml) water**
1	**tablespoon sugar**
2	**packages yeast**
5½	**cups (1,510 ml) white flour, divided**
2	**teaspoons salt**
¼	**teaspoon baking soda**
2	**tablespoons cornmeal**

1. Heat the milk and water in a medium-size pan until just below the boiling point. Add the sugar and stir until it's dissolved. Let cool until the mixture is lukewarm (95° to 110°F; 35°–40°C), then stir in the yeast and proof for 5 minutes.

2. Combine 3 cups of the flour with the salt and baking soda. Add to the liquid mixture and beat until well combined. (You can do this beating with a mixer, hand-held or otherwise, or by hand.) Now add the rest of the flour and beat again.

3. Grease two 5-cup (1,175 ml) pans and sprinkle them with the cornmeal. Using a spoon, divide the batter between the two pans. Cover and let rise until doubled.

4. Preheat your oven to 400°F (205°C). Bake the loaves for 25 minutes.

5. Remove the loaves from the pans immediately. (You may have to run a knife around the inside of the pans in order to do this.) Let them cool on a rack.

MAKES 2 FAIRLY SMALL LOAVES

BRIOCHE BREAD

The brioche dough of France can be made into a marvelous loaf of bread. A food processor makes this remarkably simple, but the bread can certainly be made by hand as well. It toasts wonderfully, and can also be used to great effect for little tea sandwiches or appetizers. (The late James Beard made a little appetizer that was much admired by putting slivers of raw onion between small circles of brioche bread and rolling the edges first in mayonnaise, then in chopped parsley.)

1	package dry yeast
¼	cup lukewarm (95° to 110°F; 35°–40°C) milk
1	tablespoon sugar
2½	cups white flour
1½	teaspoons salt
½	cup (1 stick) cold butter, cut into 8 pieces
2	eggs

1. Proof the yeast in the warm milk with the sugar.

2. Meanwhile, put the flour and salt in the food processor bowl. Buzz for a second. Add the butter and run the machine just until the mixture looks like coarse cornmeal. Pour in the yeast mixture and process very briefly. Now add the eggs and process until the dough forms a ball. (To make the dough without a food processor, cut the butter into the flour with a pastry blender or two knives. Add the yeast mixture. Beat the eggs lightly and stir those in, too.)

3. Let rise, covered, in a greased bowl until doubled in size, which will be in about 1½ hours. Punch down, knead a time or two, and shape into a loaf.

4. Put into a well-greased 5-cup loaf pan (1,175 ml: a Pyrex bread pan is this size). Let rise again, covered, until doubled — about 1 hour.

5. Preheat oven to 350°F (177°C). Bake the loaf for about 40 minutes.

MAKES 1 FAIRLY SMALL LOAF

FRENCH BREAD

A true French bread will go stale in about half a day, because it contains no fat. So that's not the sort of recipe I'm giving you. This bread might as well be called Italian (and it does make a wonderful garlic bread). So call it whatever you want! The ice cube trick will give you somewhat of an approximation of a French baker's oven, and I think you'll find that it's fun to do.

I make this in a food processor, putting the flour and salt into the bowl, then adding first the yeast mixture, then the combination of the rest of the water and butter.

1½	packages (or a scant 3½ teaspoons) dry yeast
4	teaspoons lukewarm (95° to 110°F; 35°–40°C) water
¼	teaspoon sugar
1	cup (235 ml) cold or room-temperature water
2	tablespoons butter
3½	cups (965 ml) white flour
1	teaspoon salt
2	tablespoons cornmeal

1. Proof the yeast in the warm water along with the sugar.

2. Put the cold or room-temperature water and butter into a small saucepan and slowly heat just until the butter has melted. Cool briefly. Combine all the ingredients except the cornmeal, then knead well, form into a ball, and allow to rise, covered, in a greased bowl until doubled.

3. Punch down, knead briefly, and let rise again in the greased bowl.

4. Punch down again and form the dough into a loaf that's about 13 inches (32.5 cm) long. Sprinkle the cornmeal on a baking sheet. Place the loaf on this and let it rise once more.

5. Preheat your oven to 450°F (232°C).

6. Using a very sharp knife or single-edge razor blade, cut three long diagonal slashes in the top of the loaf. Put the baking sheet in the oven.

7. Immediately throw four ice cubes onto the oven floor. (This will create the steam that would be present in a French baker's oven.) After 5 minutes, throw in four more ice cubes. Ten minutes after that, turn the oven down to 400°F (205°C) and bake for about 20 minutes more.

8. Cool on a rack.

MAKES 1 LOAF

BOULES

A boule is just a round loaf of French bread. Make French bread dough as in the above recipe, letting it rise twice. Divide it in two. One at a time, form the halves into round balls. You want to create a tight skin on each ball, so stretch it tight in all directions, tucking it under as you go. Slash an x in the top of each loaf and continue as in the French Bread recipe.

BAGUETTES

A baguette is just another French Bread variation. In this case, the loaves are smaller in diameter. As for Boules, make French Bread dough and let it rise twice. Divide it in two. If you have French bread pans, by all means use them; otherwise, you'll have to improvise. Using heavy-duty foil, doubled over, make two cradles for the bread. Let the loaves rise in their little beds, then slash their tops as for French Bread and continue as in the basic recipe, baking for 40 minutes at 300°F (150°C).

PORTUGUESE SWEET BREAD

If you live in New England, you can probably buy Portuguese Sweet Bread in a supermarket, since so many Portuguese sailors and their families ended up living in that region. (Your own will be better, though.) It's not the sort of "sweet bread" you might expect — just a light and delicious egg bread.

1	package dry yeast
½	cup (140 ml) plus 1 teaspoon sugar
¼	cup lukewarm (95° to 110°F; 35°–40°C) water
¼	cup (½ stick) soft butter
¼	cup (60 ml) warm milk
2	eggs, lightly beaten
1½	teaspoons salt
2¼	cups (620 ml) or more white flour

1. Proof the yeast with 1 teaspoon of sugar and the warm water in a large bowl.

2. Meanwhile, combine the butter with the warm milk in a small bowl, then add the rest of the sugar and mix well. Add this to the yeast mixture and stir well. Remove and reserve about one fourth of

the beaten eggs; add the rest to the mixture in the large bowl, along with the salt.

3. Add 2 cups (550 ml) of the flour, 1 cup (275 ml) at a time, mixing it in with your hands right in the bowl. Move it to a floured surface and keep on kneading, adding more flour as needed, until the dough is smooth and elastic.

4. Put in a buttered bowl, covered, to rise until doubled.

5. Punch down and shape into a ball. Put into a 9-inch (22.5 cm) buttered ovenproof skillet or a large bread pan. Cover (but not tightly) and allow to double again.

6. Preheat your oven to 350°F (177°C).

7. Brush the top of the loaf with the remaining beaten egg and bake for about half an hour.

MAKES 1 LARGE LOAF

CHALLAH

There are many ways to describe Challah. It's an egg bread. It's a braided bread. It's a ceremonial bread for Jews — and just an excellent bread for all others.

If you're not worried for religious reasons about combining meat and dairy products at the same meal, you can make your Challah with milk instead of water, and butter instead of margarine.

3	packages yeast
1⅓	cups (315 ml) lukewarm (95° to 110°F; 35°–40°C) water
1	tablespoon sugar
3	tablespoons softened margarine
1	tablespoon salt
4	eggs
5	cups (1,375 ml) or a bit more white flour
1	tablespoon water
	Poppy seeds

1. Proof the yeast in the warm water in a large bowl along with the sugar.

2. Stir in the margarine, salt, and three of the eggs, one at a time. Now add the flour, 1 cup (275 ml) at a time. You will have a very stiff dough.

3. Turn out the dough onto a floured surface and knead for about 10 minutes, until it is smooth and elastic.

4. Place the dough in a large greased bowl, turning it so it is greased on all sides. Cover and let rise until doubled in size.

5. Punch down the dough and divide it into six sections of equal size.

6. Working with one section of dough at a time, roll it out on your floured surface between your hands to make a rope that's about 1 inch (2.5 cm) in diameter.

7. Take three of these ropes and braid them into a loaf, pinching it to seal at the top and bottom and tucking the ends under. Place the loaf on a greased baking sheet.

8. Repeat with the remaining three ropes of dough. Place this loaf on the same baking sheet if there's enough room — there should be about 6 inches (15 cm) between the loaves.

9. Cover lightly and allow to rise again until almost doubled. Preheat your oven to 400°F (205°C).

10. Combine the remaining egg with the 1 tablespoon of water and brush the loaves with this egg wash. Sprinkle with poppy seeds.

11. Bake for 35 to 40 minutes.

MAKES 2 LOAVES

POTATO BREAD

Potato Bread makes lovely toast, and can also be used for sandwiches. It has a subtle taste that most people (including me) find delicious.

1	large baking potato, peeled and cut into large chunks
1	cup (235 ml) milk
3	tablespoons butter
1½	teaspoons salt
1	tablespoon sugar
1	tablespoon dry yeast
⅓	cup lukewarm (95° to 110°F; 35°–40°C) water
5	cups (1,375 ml) white flour

1. Boil the potato until soft. Drain it, but reserve the cooking liquid. Put the potato through a ricer or food mill.

2. Combine the milk with ½ cup of the potato water in a medium-size saucepan. Bring to a simmer. Remove from the fire. Add the potato and the butter, salt, and sugar. Set aside to cool to room temperature.

3. Proof the yeast in the lukewarm water, then add it to the cooled potato mixture.

4. Stir in the flour, then turn out the dough onto a floured surface and knead until it's smooth and shiny.

5. Put the dough in a greased bowl. Cover and let rise until almost doubled in size, then punch it down and turn it out onto your floured surface. Form it into a loaf, and put it into a greased 9-inch (22.5 cm) bread pan.

6. Let the dough rise again, lightly covered. Preheat your oven to 350°F (177°C).

7. Bake for 30 minutes.

MAKES 1 LARGE LOAF

Wheat and Other Grains

If you limit yourself to making white breads, you miss out on a whole bunch of healthy, hearty breads that are just as easy and forgiving as white breads are.

HEARTY WHEAT BREAD

This is an old German-influenced recipe, but it fits right in with today's ideas of how to eat — there's no fat and no sugar!

1	package dry yeast
1½	cups lukewarm (95° to 110°F; 35°–40°C) water
1	teaspoon salt
3	cups (825 ml) whole-wheat flour
1	cup (275 ml) white flour

1. Proof the yeast in the warm water in a large bowl.

2. Add the remaining ingredients and knead on a floured surface. Grease a bowl, or spray it with nonfat cooking spray; let the dough rise there, covered, until doubled.

3. Form into a loaf and place in a roughly 8 x 4-inch (20 x 10 cm) bread pan. Cover. Allow to rise again.

4. Preheat your oven to 375°F (190°C). Bake the loaf 25 to 30 minutes.

MAKES 1 FAIRLY SMALL LOAF

KATIE'S BULGUR BREAD

Here's a robust and tasty Middle European type of bread, with a few additions by a clever cook, my daughter Katie Doherty.

Bulgur is the same thing as cracked wheat, so you could call this bread that, if you like. Bulgur just sounds a bit more exotic.

1	cup (275 ml) bulgur wheat
3	tablespoons butter
1½	cups (355 ml) boiling broth (chicken, beef, or vegetable)
1¼	cups (295 ml) cold water
2	teaspoons salt
¼	cup (60 ml) honey
¼	cup (60 ml) molasses
1	teaspoon caraway seeds
1	package dry yeast
¾	cup (180 ml) lukewarm (95° to 110°F; 35°–40°C) water
3	cups (825 ml) whole-wheat flour
3	cups (825 ml) white flour

1. Put the bulgur wheat and butter in a large bowl. Stir in the boiling broth and let sit for half an hour. Add the cold water, salt, honey, molasses, and caraway.

2. Proof the yeast in the warm water and add to the bulgur mixture.

3. Now stir in the whole-wheat and white flours and knead well. Let the dough rise until fully doubled, then shape into two loaves. Put in greased 8 x 4-inch (20 x 10 cm) bread pans. Let rise again until the dough reaches the tops of the pans.

4. Preheat your oven to 375°F (190°C). Bake the loaves for 40 to 45 minutes.

Makes 2 loaves

FEEL-GOOD 100% WHOLE-WHEAT BREAD

When I have some of this bread, toasted, for breakfast, I find that I feel full of energy and generally good all day long! (So, obviously, I should have some every day . . .) This effect is heightened when I grind the wheat berries myself and use them right away. If you have a flour mill and can do this, use 2 ¾ cups (755 ml) of wheat berries, preferably hard wheat.

This recipe is different from others in this bulletin in several ways. The main thing is that you don't proof the yeast. Also, I'm giving you the recipe as I make it myself, in a food processor. No processor? I know you can figure it out! (Here's a hint: If you don't use a processor, you will have to do some kneading.)

3¾	cups (1,030 ml) whole-wheat flour (see above)
1	package yeast
1½	teaspoons salt
2	tablespoons salad oil
2	tablespoons molasses
1	tablespoon honey
1¾	cups (410 ml) lukewarm (95° to 110°F; 35°–40°C) water

1. Put the flour, yeast, and salt into the bowl of a food processor. Pulse quickly.

2. Add the rest of the ingredients and run the processor until everything is well mixed. The dough will be somewhat moist.

3. Spoon the dough into a buttered 5-cup (1,175 ml) bread pan (that's the size of the standard Pyrex pans). Cover and let rise just until the dough reaches the edge of the pan.

4. Preheat your oven to 350°F (177°C). Bake for 45 minutes.

Makes 1 small loaf

BASIC MIXED-GRAIN BREAD

Here you can add whatever pleases you. Make a three-grain bread, a five-grain one, or whatever you like. One suggestion: Keep a written record of what you use and how you feel it works out, so you'll be able to repeat your favorite combinations (although there's a lot to be said for constantly trying new flavors, too).

1	package dry yeast
2	cups (475 ml) lukewarm (95° to 110°F; 35°–40°C) water (or use milk for half of this)
2	tablespoons honey or sugar
1½	cups (415 ml) (total) any combination of: cornmeal, barley flour (or pearl barley, soaked or parboiled), raw oats, millet, triticale, quinoa, rice flour, soaked or sprouted wheat berries — whatever you want! (Or use a mixed-grain cereal from a health-food store or co-op.)
1	tablespoon salt
2	cups (550 ml) whole-wheat flour
3	cups (825 ml) white flour

1. Proof the yeast in the warm water with the honey in a large bowl.

2. Stir in the combination of grains and the salt, then the whole-wheat flour and 2 cups (550 ml) of the white flour.

3. Turn out onto a floured surface and knead in the rest of the white flour.

4. Let rise in a greased bowl, covered, until doubled.

5. Punch down. Shape into two loaves and place in greased 8½ x 4½-inch (21 x 11 cm) pans. Let rise until doubled again.

6. Preheat your oven to 350°F (177°C).

7. Bake for about 1 hour.

MAKES 2 FAIRLY SMALL LOAVES

SWEDISH RYE BREAD

In Sweden this rye bread is known as limpa. *The main things that set it apart from other ryes are the touch of orange peel and some special spices. You'll find it mainly in Midwestern kitchens and bakeries in this country.*

2	packages dry yeast
¼	cup (60 ml) lukewarm (95° to 110°F; 35°–40°c) water
¼	cup (60 ml) molasses
⅓	cup (90 ml) brown sugar
¼	cup (½ stick) butter, cut in 4 pieces
1	tablespoon salt
	Grated zest of 1 large orange
2	teaspoons anise seeds
1	teaspoon fennel seeds (optional, but good)
2	teaspoons caraway seeds (optional)
1¾	cups (410 ml) boiling water
3	cups (825 ml) rye flour
3	cups (825 ml) white flour (or a little less)
3	tablespoons milk

1. Using a small bowl, proof the yeast in the warm water along with a pinch of the brown sugar you'll be using later.

2. Put the molasses, brown sugar, butter, salt, orange peel, and whatever seeds you're using into a big bowl. Add the boiling water and stir. When this has cooled to lukewarm, add the yeast mixture.

3. Now stir in first the rye flour, then most of the white. Turn out onto a floured surface. Knead for about 10 minutes, adding the rest of the white flour if necessary. Put into a buttered or oiled bowl, turning the dough so all sides will be greased.

4. Cover. Let stand in a warm place until doubled. Punch down, cover, and let rise again. (This step is optional, but helps the texture.)

5. Shape into two oval loaves, each 12 to 14 inches (30–35 cm) long. Put onto a lightly greased baking sheet. Cover and let rise once more. (Don't place them too close together, as the loaves will spread.)

6. Preheat your oven to 375°F (190°C).

7. When the loaves have doubled in size, slash their tops diagonally in several places, French bread–style. Bake for 25 to 30 minutes. Brush tops of the loaves with the milk, then allow them to cool on a rack.

MAKES 2 LOAVES

CARAWAY RYE BATTER BREAD

This recipe is primarily for those who don't find that kneading is necessary to their mental health, but it's also a nice bread that you'll be proud to make.

If you don't want a caraway rye bread, just (guess what?) omit the caraway seeds.

2	**packages yeast**
4	**tablespoons sugar, divided**
1	**cup (235 ml) lukewarm (95° to 110°F; 35°–40°C) water**
1	**cup (235 ml) milk**
1	**egg**
¼	**cup (60 ml) salad oil**
1	**tablespoon salt**
2	**tablespoons caraway seeds**
2	**cups (550 ml) rye flour**
1½–2 cups (415–550 ml) white flour	

1. Proof the yeast along with 1 tablespoon of the sugar in the warm water in a large bowl.

2. Add the milk, egg, salad oil, and salt. Combine well.

3. Combine the rye and white flours, then stir the caraway seeds and the remaining sugar into the flour. Beat into the liquid mixture, 1 cup at a time, the rye flour, then enough of the white flour to make a stiff batter.

4. Cover the bowl and allow the batter to rise for 30 minutes (it should not double in size).

5. Stir down the batter, then spoon it into two 8 x 4-inch (20 x 10 cm) bread pans.

6. Preheat your oven to 375°F (190°C). When the batter in the pans has risen just slightly (about 15 minutes), put them in the oven. Bake for 35 to 40 minutes, then remove from the pans at once and allow to cool on a rack.

MAKES 2 SMALL LOAVES

RAISIN PUMPERNICKEL BREAD

Raisin Pumpernickel is a New York tradition. It's quite black in color and quite delicious to taste. You can make it into great sandwiches (for instance, try one with ripe Brie and prosciutto) or just eat it by the slice.

1	**package dry yeast**
¾	**cup (180 ml) lukewarm (95° to 110°F; 35°–40°C) water**
¼	**cup (60 ml) molasses**
1½	**teaspoons salt**
1	**tablespoon dry cocoa**
1	**teaspoon instant coffee granules**
1	**cup (275 ml) rye flour**
1	**cup (275 ml) white flour**
1	**cup (275 ml) whole-wheat flour**
½	**cup (140 ml) raisins**
2	**tablespoons cornmeal**

Egg wash (1 egg beaten with 2 tablespoons water)

1. Proof the yeast in the water with the molasses.

2. Stir the salt, cocoa, and coffee granules into the rye flour, then stir this into the yeast mixture. Mix well.

3. Combine the white and whole-wheat flours, and add about 1½ cups (415 ml) of this to the yeast and rye flour mixture.

4. Turn out onto a floured board and knead in the rest of the flour. Let the dough rise in a greased bowl, covered, until doubled; this may take an hour or even two.

5. Punch the dough down. Put the raisins onto your floured board, plop out the dough onto this, and knead well, until the raisins are well incorporated. Let the rough rise again, then shape into a round loaf.

6. Sprinkle the cornmeal on a baking sheet and place the loaf on it. Let it rise, covered, until doubled once again.

7. Preheat your oven to 375°F (190°C).

8. Cut across the top of the loaf in two or three places with a single-edge razor or a sharp knife. Brush with the egg wash; wait 5 minutes and repeat.

9. Bake for 40 to 45 minutes.

MAKES 1 LOAF

HONEY OATMEAL BREAD

When you eat oatmeal bread, it's not hard at all to believe that it gives you strength and energy. After all, there's the old saying that someone is "feeling his oats." Also, horse owners and trainers are careful not to give their charges too many oats lest they become rambunctious!

This bread is at its best when made with a steel-cut variety of oats. However, any sort of uncooked oatmeal, even the "quick" type, will give you a very nice bread.

1	package dry yeast
2	cups (475 ml) lukewarm (95° to 110°F; 35°–40°C) water
¼	cup honey
2	teaspoons salt
4	cups (1,100 ml) flour
1	cup (275 ml) uncooked oatmeal
3	tablespoons melted butter

1. Proof the yeast in a combination of the water and honey in a large bowl.

2. Combine the salt, flour, and oatmeal and add to the proofed yeast along with the butter.

3. Turn out onto a floured surface and knead.

4. Put into a greased bowl. Cover and let rise until doubled in size.

5. Turn out again onto the floured surface and punch down. Shape into a loaf. Put into a fairly large greased loaf pan. Cover loosely and let sit until doubled in size again.

6. Preheat your oven to 375°F (190°C).

7. Bake for about 40 minutes.

MAKES 1 LARGE LOAF

Specialty Breads

Unique flavors, special ingredients, and new techniques give these breads their special flavors.

ONION BREAD

When I lived in Manhattan, a bakery near me made an onion bread I had a hard time resisting. Now I no longer live there, but I've learned to make my own!

1	package dry yeast
1	cup (235 ml) lukewarm (95° to 110°F; 35°–40°C) water
2	teaspoons sugar
2	teaspoons salt, divided
3	cups (825 ml) white flour
2	tablespoons melted butter
⅔	cup (185 ml) minced onion

1. Using a large bowl, proof the yeast in the lukewarm water along with the sugar. Add 1 teaspoon of the salt.

2. Beat in 2 cups (550 ml) of the flour. When well mixed, beat in ½ cup (140 ml) more.

3. Turn out onto a board or other surface on which you have spread ½ cup (140 ml) more flour. Knead well, until all the flour has been incorporated and the dough is shiny and elastic.

4. Put in a greased bowl. Turn the dough around in it. Cover. Let rise until doubled in size, about 1 hour.

5. Punch down the dough and divide it into halves. Put each in a greased 9-inch (22.5 cm) round cake pan.

6. Brush the top of each loaf with butter and sprinkle on the onion, then, using your fingers, poke down the onion pieces into the dough. (The tops of the loaves will look dented.)

7. Let rise until doubled again (the loaves do not need to be covered).

8. Preheat your oven to 450°F (232°C) (very hot).

9. Sprinkle remaining salt on the loaves. Bake for about 20 minutes.

MAKES 2 ROUND LOAVES

CHEESE BREAD

You probably won't be able to buy cheese bread anywhere, but making your own is a snap — and a highly worthwhile way to spend your time! You'll love it plain or toasted, or as the base for an appetizer, or made into croutons, or . . .

1	package dry yeast
1	tablespoon sugar
½	cup (120 ml) lukewarm (95° to 110°F; 35°–40°C) water
1¼	cups (295 ml) milk
2½	cups (690 ml) grated or shredded Cheddar cheese
3	tablespoons salad oil
1½	teaspoons salt
5–6	cups (1,375–1,650 ml) white flour

1. Proof the yeast in a large bowl along with the sugar in the lukewarm water.

2. Beat in the milk, cheese, and oil, then add the salt and 2½ cups (690 ml) of the flour and mix well.

3. Add another 2½ cups (690 ml) of flour and turn out onto a well-floured surface. Knead until smooth and shiny, adding more flour if necessary.

4. Put the dough in a greased bowl, turning it around, then cover and let it rise until doubled in size.

5. Punch down the dough and divide it in two. Shape into two loaves and place them in greased 9-inch (22.5 cm) bread pans. Cover lightly and let rise again until once more doubled. Preheat your oven to 350°F (177°C).

6. Bake for about 40 minutes.

MAKES 2 LARGE LOAVES

ANADAMA BATTER BREAD

On the faint chance that you don't know the story, Anadama Bread is supposed to have been invented by a long-ago man who returned home after a hard day's work to find his wife, Anna, not there, and nothing ready for his dinner except cornmeal mush. "Anna, damn her!" he cried, we're told, then threw some molasses, flour, and another thing or two into the mush and proceeded to make this wonderful bread.

Pepperidge Farm used to market Anadama Bread under the name Corn and Molasses Bread. I was a faithful customer. Now I have to make my own, but it's not at all hard, so I don't mind too much. Try it yourself!

I'm giving you a batter-bread version. It works well, and seems to me to carry out the "Anna, damn her!" story. I've made other versions, including some that contain whole wheat, and they just don't seem quite the same.

1	package dry yeast
¼	cup (60 ml) lukewarm (95° to 110°F; 35°–40°C) water
¾	cup (180 ml) boiling water
½	cup (140 ml) cornmeal
3	tablespoons room-temperature butter
¼	cup molasses
1½	teaspoons salt
1	egg
2¾	cups (755ml) white flour, divided

1. Proof the yeast in the lukewarm water in a small bowl.

2. In a large bowl (preferably one that goes with an electric mixer), combine the boiling water, cornmeal, butter, molasses, and salt. Let cool to about 100 degrees. Stir in the proofed yeast and the egg.

3. Add 1½ cups (415 ml) of the flour and beat until well combined, either by machine or by hand (or in a food processor). Now add the rest of the flour and beat again.

4. Spoon the dough into a greased 9-inch (22.5 cm) bread pan. Let rise until it reaches just partway up the pan — about 1 inch (2.5 cm) from the top will be fine. Preheat your oven to 375°F (190°C).

5. Bake for about 35 minutes.

MAKES 1 LARGE LOAF

MONKEY BREAD

I've read that Nancy Reagan insisted Monkey Bread be served at most White House dinners when she was the first lady. An odd choice, many thought, but there's no getting around the fact that it is quite delicious!

2	packages dry yeast
1	cup (275 ml) white (granulated) sugar
½	cup (120 ml) lukewarm (95° to 110°F; 35°–40°C) water
1	cup (2 sticks) room-temperature butter, divided
1½	tablespoons salt
1	cup (235 ml) lukewarm (95° to 110°F; 35°–40°C) milk
4	eggs (or 3 eggs and 2 egg yolks)
6	cups (1,650 ml) or more white flour
½	cup (140 ml) light brown sugar

1. Proof the yeast along with the white sugar in the lukewarm water in a large bowl.

2. Stir half the butter (that's 1 stick) and the salt into the warm milk. Don't worry if it doesn't completely dissolve. Add this to the proofed yeast mixture. Add the eggs. Mix very thoroughly.

3. Now start adding the flour, 1 cup (275 ml) at a time, mixing it in well each time. After about 5 cups (1,375 ml), the dough will become rather difficult to handle, so turn it out on a well-floured surface and add more flour until you have a dough that is no longer sticky and can be kneaded. This may take another 2 cups (550 ml) of flour (making a total of 7 cups; 1,925 ml).

4. Knead very thoroughly, until the dough is absolutely manageable. Put it into a greased bowl, turning to coat it all over. Cover and let rise until doubled in size. Punch down the dough. Let it rest for 5 minutes, then turn it out onto a lightly floured surface.

5. Let the dough rest where it is while you melt the remaining stick of butter and combine it with the brown sugar.

6. Now comes the fun: Make the dough into balls the size of Ping-Pong balls. Working with one a time, dip the balls into the brown sugar mixture and place in a well-buttered tube pan (like an angel food cake pan). There should be some of the brown sugar mixture left; just pour it over the top of the pan.

7. Cover the pan loosely and allow the dough to rise once more, this time to the top of the pan. Preheat your oven to 375°F (190°C).

8. Bake for an hour or a few minutes more. Test for doneness by tapping the top of the bread — if it's done, it will sound hollow. Turn out of the pan onto a plate.

9. If you serve the bread warm, you and your guests can pull off little globes of dough. Otherwise, the bread can be cooled and sliced. I have no idea which way it was served in the White House, but suspect that, at least for formal dinners, it was sliced.

MAKES 1 VERY LARGE LOAF

Unleavened Bread — The Kaleidoscope

Kaleidoscope Bread is so called (by me) because it can contain an amazing number of good things — dried or fresh fruits of all sorts, nuts, seeds, grains, various flours, spices, herbs, and more. A slice of it can look exotically kaleidoscopic.

I'm calling it "unleavened" bread because you don't use either yeast or baking powder to make it. There is a danger, though, that you may think it's one of the unleavened cracker-type breads such as matzo. No, there is nothing faintly resembling a cracker about this beautiful bread.

I think that you could live for a long time on nothing but this bread, and very healthily, too. (And happily!)

The basic concept comes from Julie Jordan's *Wings of Life.* I was given this book about 20 years ago, and I thought "No way" when I first read about making unleavened bread. But then my curiosity took over, and I gave it a try.

Ms. Jordan had promised breads that would be moist and, in her words, "solid and unpretentious, dark brown and earthy, and when you bite into them, there's really something there." She was absolutely right. These are the most satisfying breads you can possibly imagine.

There's only one place I would quarrel with her. She says to beware of undercooking the loaves — that if you aren't careful, you'll end up with loaves with uncooked centers. Maybe, but the only calamity I've had with these breads occurred the one time I overcooked them. The result: cannonballs.

My proportions are fairly different from hers — but after all, she does encourage you to do whatever appeals to you in making these breads. So although I'll be giving you amounts that I like to use, you don't have to be a copycat.

First, I'll list the basic ingredients; then I'll give you a specific recipe of my own devising that has worked out well for me.

Flour. Whole wheat. White. Rye. Cornmeal. Any other flour you can think of or locate — soy, millet, buckwheat, and so on.

Liquid. Water, milk, yogurt, the liquid in which you've cooked vegetables (especially potatoes) . . . anything wet!

Something sweet. Honey's good, as are molasses and maple syrup. Sugar will do, too, especially raw sugar.

Sea salt.

Cooked grains. These are optional, but they do add a nice body and flavor to your bread, plus some moistness. You can choose from brown rice, wheat berries, oatmeal, and more.

Fruit, nuts, and seeds. If you use fresh fruit such as bananas or plums, you're adding extra moisture, which never (within reason!) does any harm. Dried fruit helps add a certain amount of moisture, too, and gives your bread extra texture and flavor. It also creates the kaleidoscope effect — just think of little nuggets of, say, dried apricots or dried cranberries showing up in a slice of bread. Nuts (and you can add any you can possibly think of) add their own magic, as do seeds.

Spices and herbs. Once again, use whatever you're especially fond of. I tend to use gentle spices such as dry coriander, though a touch of cinnamon and/or nutmeg can be delightful.

Oils. You need a small amount of oil to add softness to your unleavened bread. My personal preference these days is extra-virgin olive oil, but you can also use soy, canola, or peanut oil, and walnut oil is a special treat.

KALEIDOSCOPE BREAD

As promised, here is a Kaleidoscope Bread I've worked out. I've listed the ingredients I love in it, though at times I've added other luscious things such as cinnamon, oatmeal, dried cranberries, and/or sunflower seeds. My comment at the time I wrote down the ingredients, after baking and tasting the bread: "Stupendous!"

I make the dough in a food processor, but many of you will prefer to mix the ingredients together, then knead very thoroughly.

4	cups (1,100 ml) whole-wheat flour
½	cup (140 ml) seven-grain cereal
1	cup (275 ml) cornmeal
1½	ripe bananas
1½	cups (415 ml) raisins
1	cup (275 ml) cut-up apricots
½	cup (140 ml) chopped cashews
2	tablespoons walnut oil
2	teaspoons sea salt
2	tablespoons honey
1	tablespoon molasses
1	teaspoon dry coriander
2	teaspoons poppy seeds
1½	cups (355 ml) hot water

1. Combine all the ingredients. If you use a food processor, put the flours and cornmeal in first. Otherwise, it's a good plan to combine all the other ingredients, then stir in the flours.

2. With a food processor, after mixing the ingredients together, run the machine until a firm but malleable and moist dough is formed. By hand, knead and knead and knead.

3. Form the dough into two round balls. Place them on a lightly oiled baking sheet and, using a sharp knife, slash a cross-hatch on the top of each ball.

4. What happens next is up to you. You can bake your loaves right away or you can let them sit for a few hours, even a day. According to Julie Jordan, there are people who feel that a natural leavening takes place if the dough is allowed to rest a bit. She hasn't observed this herself, though, and neither have I. But maybe you will!

5. Before you want to bake, whenever that is, preheat your oven to 350°F (177°C).

6. Bake the loaves until the crust is firm and a medium brown color. Remove to a rack to cool. For me, using these ingredients, this takes 50 minutes. Ms. Jordan uses at least 5 cups (1,375 ml) of flour and 3 cups (705 ml) of liquid and feels that the loaves require 1¼ to 1½ hours.

MAKES TWO 1½-POUND (680 g) LOAVES

Sources for Flours, Grains, Mills, and Many Et Ceteras

King Arthur
800-827-6836
www.kingarthurflour.com
For flour and grains, mills and storage canisters, and all sorts of bread-making gear, try good old King Arthur. They'll send you a comprehensive catalog, or if you're in the Northeast, you can go to their store in Norwich, Vermont. (Their main flours, the unbleached all-purpose Special for Machines Bread Flour and 100% White Whole Wheat, are also available in many supermarkets in the United States.)

Bob's Red Mill
800-349-2173
www.bobsredmill.com
Bob's Red Mill carries not only excellent flours and grains but also wonderful baking mixes and hot cereals. Their top sellers include their 5 Grain Rolled Cereal and Whole Wheat Pastry Flour, but in total they have hundreds of products for bakers, many organic. Long a health-food-store staple, Bob's Red Mill's products are now available in many supermarkets.

Hodgson Mill
800-347-0105
www.hodgsonmill.com
This family-owned company from the Ozarks produces great flours and other vital ingredients for bakers; they also produce baking mixes (including a delicious Whole-Grain Gingerbread), plus whole wheat pasta and couscous. Their philosophy is "premium quality, nothing added, nothing taken away." Shop on-line, or look for them at mainstream supermarkets and health-food stores.

Nothing beats freshly ground flour. For a flour mill of your own:

Bears In The Woods Products,
866-339-5060, *www.bearsinthewoods.net*
Pleasant Hill Grain, 800-321-1073, *www.pleasanthillgrain.com*
The Country Living Grain Mill,
340-652-0671, *www.countrylivinggrainmills.com*